ALFRED CHESTER BEATTY

FROM MINER TO BIBLIOPHILE

D1194693

About the author

Charles Horton has nearly twenty years experience in working for museums and specialist historical collections in Ireland. After completing his primary and postgraduate studies at Trinity College Dublin and University College Dublin, he completed further postgraduate study at University College London. His specialised interests include the history of the book and, in particular, the history of book collecting. He has been the Curator of the Western Collections of the Chester Beatty Library since 1990.

ALFRED CHESTER BEATTY

From Miner to Bibliophile

Charles Horton

TOWN
HOUSE
DUBLIN

First published in 2003 by
TownHouse, Dublin
THCH Ltd
Trinity House
Charleston Road
Ranelagh
Dublin 6
Ireland

1 2 3 4 5 6 7 8 9 10

A CIP catalogue record for this book is available from the
British Library.

ISBN: 1-86059-163-9

Cover and text design by Wendy Williams Design
Typeset by Wendy Williams Design
Printed by Nørhaven Book, Denmark

Contents

Although various aspects of the life of Alfred Chester Beatty (1875–1968), American mining engineer, industrialist and collector, have been published, the history of Beatty as a book collector has yet to be written. Beatty assembled a large and choice collection of manuscripts, printed books and prints, comprising the ancient, mediaeval and modern, as well as the rare, unusual and even the bizarre from both the occidental and oriental worlds. Collected over sixty years, the Beatty collection was regarded in the 1950s as one of the finest private collections held in England.

But who was Beatty and was he any different from other American book collectors of the early-20th century? The many published works that list book collectors and their achievements often fail to mention him.[1] His early life and initial collecting activities were centred in the United States and, accordingly, one might expect to find his name included amongst those of the great American collectors such as Henry E Huntington (1850–1927), J Pierpont Morgan (1837–1913) and Henry Folger (1857–1930). This is not the case, however, since Beatty's move to London in 1911 had removed him from the milieu of those involved in what has been called the 'golden years of American collecting'. The development of Beatty's library in the 1920s and 1930s, after he had settled in England, might lead one to expect that he would be included in a list of great English book collectors like Henry Yates Thompson (1838–1928), Sir George Holford (1860–1926) or Charles Dyson Perrins (1864–1958), but such exalted ranks were still closed to the "Boches, Jews, and Transatlantics".[2]

Beatty was, in many respects, an extraordinary man. Although a member of the Sons of the Revolution, he regarded himself as an adopted son of the British Empire.[3] He developed mining enterprises in the United States, Central America, Europe, Africa and Asia and, from the wealth created by these enterprises, he endowed museums with gifts, sponsored academics and built, at his own expense, the Chester Beatty Research Institute for Cancer at the Royal Marsden Hospital, London. He was a Republican and a Tory in politics and a personal friend of Herbert Hoover and Sir Winston Churchill. He was described in one account as having been "cast in a heroic mould" with "a Churchillian sweep and a supreme contempt of every kind of socialist bureaucracy". Reporting the news of his death in 1968, *The Times* lamented that "the world has lost one of its most romantic characters".

The Formative Years 1875–1910

Beatty was born in New York on 7 February 1875 into a family that united Ulster-Scots, English and Irish ancestry.[4] In later life, he recalled his early schoolboy habit of collecting mineral specimens and of attending auctions and buying at market stalls.[5] He vividly recalled his first attendance, aged ten, at Bangs & Company Auction House on Broadway. Accompanied by his father, he had spotted a piece of pink calcite that he wanted for his mineral collection and, armed with his 15 cents savings, he sat through the auction until his lot came up for sale.

STAMP COLLECTION Chester Beatty's stamp collection was no mere boyhood hobby. His collection of the earliest stamps and postal history covers won him the Tilleard Medal from the Royal Philatelic Society, London (1945) and prizes at the New York Philatelic Club (1947). Beatty sold most of his stamp collection but several hundred postal items still remain in the library.

" 'How much am I bid?' asked the auctioneer. 'Ten cents,' came the boy's instantaneous response before any potential bidder had a chance to open his mouth. The auctioneer grinned incredulously. 'What more am I bid, gentlemen?' he urged. With nervous tension, the boy was praying inwardly that nobody would dare to increase the bidding. 'Any advance?' coaxed the auctioneer with increasing apprehension as the crowd remained silent. 'Now, gentlemen, surely this beautiful specimen is worth more than ten cents.' The auctioneer pleaded in vain. 'You men are outbid by babes and sucklings', was the auctioneer's parting crack as he joined the crowd in laughter." [6]

Beatty's schoolboy interest in minerals, and some paternal advice from a family friend, led him to pursue, from 1894–98, an engineering degree at

Columbia University's School of Mines. After qualifying, he headed west for Denver, Colorado, situated at the head of many of the mining trails that made the area one of the most important mining centres in the United States. Mining settlements at the foot of the Rocky Mountains (such as Leadville, Boulder, Cripple Creek, and Matchless) had changed little in the fifteen years since Oscar Wilde had descended the 300 feet (91 metres) to the bottom of a mineshaft in 1882 to deliver a lecture to local miners on the value of aesthetics.[7] These towns were still full of people trying to make a fortune from the mineral resources of the area and Beatty was just another individual in search of such a fortune. At first, his academic qualifications were of little use and he was obliged to take a job for $2 a day as a 'mucker', clearing away rock and soil from the mine tunnels and living in the camp bunkhouse. Within a few months, however, Beatty was offered the position of mine superintendent but, in the following year, he decided to establish his own consultancy and thereafter spent most of his time exposing 'salted' mines and fraudulent deposit claims. Later, in 1900,

BEATTY THE MINER *(ON RIGHT)* Beatty's mining career began as the era of the American Wild West was ending. In 1898 he worked in the gold fields of Colorado and later in the silver mines of the Sierra Madre, Mexico. By 1908, and already a millionaire, he had established himself as one of the leading mining consultants in America. In later years, his mining interests included lead mines in Yugoslavia, copper mines in Northern Rhodesia (Zambia) and diamond mines in Sierra Leone. By the 1950s he was known in the popular press as the 'World's Copper King'.

he headed for the gold mines of Cripple Creek, Colorado, then the largest gold-producing area in the world. Gradually his earnings increased to $1,200 per year, prompting his observation, "I still have beer tastes but I hope to get to champagne some day."[8]

Beatty and the Golden Years of American Collecting

There is no doubt that, in the field of book collecting, Beatty's activities were immense, giving rise to over fifty multi-volume catalogues or handlists and numerous monographs. Like many American book collectors of his generation, Beatty arranged for the establishment of his library as an institution after his death and, although it is not clear why Beatty collected, he left clear instructions as to why he wanted his collection kept intact. Not for him the feelings of Robert Hoe III (1839–1909) who decided to sell his collection: "If the great collections of the past had not been sold where would I have found my books?"[9] Some collectors, contemporary with Beatty, such as Alfred C Chapin (1848–1936), Speaker of the New York State Assembly, were determined to build "the most fully representative collection possible of those fundamental books and manuscripts which constitute the great humanistic traditions so essential to a liberal arts education".[10] Henry E Huntington wanted to assemble a library of libraries in California, while J Pierpont Morgan was so avaricious in his collecting that he bought "anything from a pyramid to the tooth of Mary Magdalene" (the reliquary of the Tooth of Saint Mary Magdalene is now in the Metropolitan Museum of Art, New York). Henry Clay Folger's collecting passion was for the complete works of Shakespeare, but he was not content to leave his great collection of Elizabethan literature for posterity: he also included his ashes, housing them in a niche in the library.[11] Beatty, however, left no statement as to why he wanted to collect books, even in later life.

Many recent studies have explored the psychological background to collecting; suggesting that, in the early decades of the 20th century, the book-collecting pursuits of many American collectors "provided for them the means which allowed them to cope with a modernizing world, in which the older Victorian cultural hegemony was under assault by the rise of mass culture and the consolidation of industrial corporate capitalism".[12] Many of the external factors and psychological characteristics that may have influenced Beatty, such as social status and personal circumstances, still remain to be examined and whether his collection was ultimately "a means to physical security, distinction, knowledge and aesthetic satisfaction"[13] is a subject that warrants future study. With Beatty, there are certainly some noticeable personal characteristics: his politics and his personal taste in art were conservative, but his relationship with his library was more complex, changing over the years as he refined his collecting. His distinct mistrust of modern art was expressed in an interview with *The Times*:

"Get a group of common artists, fill them full of champagne and vodka, furnish them with big brushes and masses of canvas. One group would scrape the paintings down, the others would daub them, and you'd evolve a new school, arrange a series of 'collections' and everyone would enthuse."[14]

The period just before World War I also saw some important economic developments, which favoured certain collectors, particularly the Americans. In 1909, the United States abolished its 20 per cent import duty on works of art over a hundred years old.[15] This change in the law prompted J Pierpont Morgan to transfer his collections from England to New York; a move that prompted a correspondence in *The Times*, as the English public became "increasingly and indignantly aware of the selling, largely by noble families, to foreigners, largely Americans, of their ancestral treasures".[16] Certainly, the books available in the auction rooms and on the shelves of dealers provided a feast for bibliophiles which, on occasions like the first session of the Hoe sale (New York, 24 April 1911), appeared more like a feeding frenzy as the great collectors vied with each other in $20,000 and $50,000 bids to secure their favourite lots.[17] This sale was described as a "battle of the Titans" where "mere demigods and heroes were outclassed" which not only lead to an outcry in the press over the extravagance, but also contributed in a considerable degree to raising the prices of rare books.[18]

Chester Beatty's Early Collections

It was against this background that Beatty's first major acquisitions were made, particularly after he had returned to New York from Denver in 1905, by which time he was a millionaire. He and his young family now travelled in style, usually requiring three cabins on board trains or ships; one for Beatty and his wife Grace, one for their two children, Ninette and Chester junior, and the third for his personal staff. His new status required a new home (5th

Avenue at East 73rd Street) and, for the first time, he included a library, which housed his early collections. These included European illuminated manuscripts, Old Master prints, English and French colour-plate books, and one Islamic item, identified only as "leaves from a Shahnama", the Persian epic poem.

Like many collectors, Chester Beatty was influenced by the tastes and collecting fashions of his era. American book collectors at the turn of the 20th century were predominantly interested in European illustrated books, particularly illuminated manuscripts or English and French colour-plate books that featured exotic costumes or animals from faraway places. Many also sought out incunabula (the books printed in Europe from the very earliest days of Gutenberg's invention), as well as the earliest editions of particular works. In his early collecting years, Beatty followed suit, collecting similar categories to the other collectors, but with the important consideration that each purchase should be value for money. The financial records surviving in the Chester Beatty archives show that, in the period before 1921, Beatty never spent more than $5,000 on any one book. Beatty continued to add to his collection, often acquiring items on several trips to Europe but, in 1911, his wife, Grace, died of typhoid fever, leaving Beatty with two young children to rear. This personal tragedy, combined with his own ill-health and his desire to become a mining financier, prompted his move from the United States to London, then the centre of international trade.

BARODA HOUSE, 24 KENSINGTON PALACE GARDENS, LONDON, c.1912
Baroda House was originally built in 1845 in the Moorish style, to the designs of Owen Jones, one of the greatest Victorian designers. It became the London residence of the Maharajah of Baroda in 1891 and was purchased by Beatty in 1912. Apart from this mansion, Beatty also purchased Calehill Park, a large estate in Kent, but during the winter months he preferred to live in Cairo (1919–39) and then, the south of France (1946–68). When he moved to Ireland in 1950, he purchased a large residence in Ballsbridge, Dublin and a country estate in County Wicklow.

In 1913, Beatty remarried. His new wife was fellow New Yorker, Edith Dunne and, a few months later, the family embarked on their first extended trip to Egypt. Cairo was then a popular winter resort for international travellers, some of whom were great collectors. Beatty found that the dry climate of Egypt so relieved his health problems that he returned there almost every year until the outbreak of World War II. Each year, the family would leave London, usually in December, for Paris, where they stayed for a few days visiting the antique shops and dealers. From Marseilles, they would then sail to Port Said and travel onwards to Cairo. The return trip would occasionally vary to include Constantinople or Naples, Rome and Venice, and these extended trips allowed Beatty to build up extensive contacts with continental and Egyptian dealers.

NINETTE AND CHESTER BEATTY JR IN EGYPT In 1919, Beatty built a villa for his family at Giza with views of the Great Pyramid. Over the years, the villa saw many important guests including Winston Churchill, who used the villa on his way to the Tehran Conference of Allied Leaders in 1943.

At the outbreak of World War I, Beatty decided to let his house in New York and stay in London. In 1915, in response to the need for humanitarian aid, he turned his London home, Baroda House, into a hospital for the American Red Cross. While generally exhorting his wife to be economical during this period of hardship, Beatty spent $54,751 on jewellery for her, as well as giving $40,000 to the Red Cross. Snuff bottles were added to the collection almost on a monthly basis, while, at the same time, he acquired more manuscripts, printed books, and Dürer prints, but only at a rate of a few thousand dollars a year. In 1917, Beatty started to increase his spending on

CHESTER BEATTY IN JAPAN Chester Beatty, his wife and daughter at a dinner party hosted by the antique dealer Yamanaka Sadajiro in Osaka, Japan, 1917.

illuminated manuscripts, purchasing several fine examples from the London firm of Quaritch's, but his greatest additions were to be made a few months later when he took his family to the Far East for the first time. Beatty and his family spent nearly six months touring China and Japan. He had already purchased some Chinese and Japanese items while living in New York, and this trip enabled Beatty to purchase some of the finest items direct from the best dealers in Osaka, Kyoto and Yokohama. Many of the receipts and customs declarations made on this trip still remain in the Chester Beatty archives, showing that over $50,000 was spent on enhancing this part of the collection. Purchases included Chinese dragon robes, imperial jade books and Japanese painted scrolls.

The Western Collections

The early collection of Western illuminated manuscripts and rare books purchased by Beatty was assembled without the guidance of a specialist advisor or dealer. Sir Sydney Cockerell, a well-known expert on mediaeval illumination and later director of the Fitzwilliam Museum, Cambridge, disapproved of the quality of Beatty's manuscripts and "hurried him at once to tea with the Yates Thompsons to see manuscripts that would raise his standards".[19] The earliest purchases were made between 1914 and 1916 and include no less than five French 15th-century Books of Hours. These manuscripts came from a variety of dealers in London as well as elsewhere, and Beatty carefully recorded the cost of each of his purchases, noting it in a code based on the letters of his country house: C.A.L.E.H.I.L. P.R.K. [Calehill Park] to represent 1.2.3.4.5.6.7.8.9.0.[20] The earliest purchases had come from famous collections that had recently been dispersed – one important manuscript had been exhibited at the Burlington Fine Arts Club – so, in many respects, they may be regarded as 'safe' purchases. Beatty, like many other collectors, often acquired works that had been previously accepted into known collections or had been on public exhibition.

By 1918, Beatty's Western collection had improved and he was now collecting very actively in this area. The London book dealer Bernard Quaritch appears as the main source for these books, which included items from the Hoe, Huth, and Fairfax Murray collections, but the most important acquisition was probably the Hours of the Emperor Charles V, with miniatures attributed at the time to Hans Memling.[21] The main sale in 1919 was that of Henry Yates Thompson's celebrated collection of illuminated manuscripts, and the veteran collector presented Beatty with a copy of the catalogue. The catalogue is heavily annotated, suggesting Beatty's interest in several items, but he was only successful in securing one manuscript, a 9th-century Latin Gospel book, the other lots selling perhaps for more than Beatty was prepared to pay. Beatty's disappointment may have been eased when, a few weeks later, he was presented with a gift from his wife of one of the most important manuscripts from the Yates Thompson collection. This was the magnificent Hours of Admiral Prigent de Coëtivy (1400–1450), soldier and bibliophile, who was slain by an English cannonball at the siege of Cherbourg in 1450.[22] This manuscript, with its 148 miniatures by the "Master of the Duke of Bedford", had been one of the best of Henry Yates Thompson's collection and it now became one of the treasures of Beatty's library.

Beatty's notebooks show that he was acquiring the confidence to grade his collection according to quality and rarity. He used a simple alphabetical code for each purchase, grading the manuscript in relation to similar examples he had seen in the British Museum, the Bibliothèque nationale, Paris, or other major museums. Each manuscript was graded A, B, C, etc., with a qualifier attached such as A+, A–, or from 1A to 50A (often expressed in Roman numerals). Beatty rarely bought C material, and, if he did, he would often sell it again. Only exceptionally would he allow B material to remain in the collection. An example of this grading can be found in some pages taken from a small pocketbook, which records Beatty's visit in February 1918 to the Bodleian Library, Oxford.

THE EMPEROR XUANZONG
LOOKS AT THE LOTUS
FLOWERS OF THE POOL
OF TAI YI
From the Chogonka Scroll
Early-17th century
Edo period
Japan
CBL J 1158

The Japanese collection of the library is particularly renowned for its painted scrolls and albums. These include the Chogonka Scroll (The Song of Everlasting Sorrow) painted by Kano Sansetsu (1590–1651). Based on a true story, it describes the Emperor Xuanzong's doomed love affair with the beautiful young concubine, Yang Guifei.

DECORATED INITIAL E
De Civitate Dei
(St Augustine)
Latin manuscript on vellum
c. 1100
CBL Ms W. 43 f.123

Although Beatty purchased Western illuminated manuscripts while he was still living in America, they are only referred to in the accounts as 'Hours' (French Books of Hours). From 1919–32 Beatty collected over 250 examples of mediaeval and Renaissance manuscripts, some of which were sold in two sales, between 1932–33 and in 1968–69, after his death.

"The Douce manuscripts in the case

[No.] 15804, Poor quality of no interest E.

[No.] 21604, Douce 30, a charming Dutch manuscript.Well worth seeing again B.

[No.] 21817, Douce 243, Interesting but not of fine quality C.

[No.] 19475, worthless E+."

Perhaps it was through these visits to museums, or conversations with other collectors like Henry Yates Thompson and Sydney Cockerell, that Beatty's preference for certain types of manuscript evolved, for in a letter dated 28 July 1919 to Martin Nijhoff, a Dutch dealer, he expresses the view:

"I do not like secular manuscripts as much as the religious ones. Also I do not care for Portulano's. Personally I think that the Portulano's in the Yates Thompson collection sold for more than they were worth.

"I would like to know if you have any fine Italian or Dutch manuscripts (religious) also if you have any fine Bibles or Breviary of any century. I prefer the early ones say XIIIth, XIVth century ones in this class of book [...] I would also like to get some of the books published by Blaue and Martin (other than atlases) which are hand coloured, or any fine books with contemporary hand colouring [...] the Book of Hours from the Huth collection that you sent me was a nice book but unfortunately, I had one very similar evidently from the same atelier."[23]

By 1919, Beatty's collection had developed from a rather unstructured and haphazard one in 1911 to a moderate-sized library, containing a substantial number of Old Master prints, early printed books and albums, European and Persian illuminated manuscripts, as well as Chinese and Japanese painted scrolls. In general, it was still an eclectic collection that, in many respects, resembled a 'cabinet of curiosities' rather than a determined collection on any particular subject or class of object.

The Development of the Collection

By the early 1920s, however, Beatty was no longer an amateur collector. His library had grown so large that he was forced to convert the conservatory

SNUFF BOTTLE
Carved Lapis lazuli
19th century
CBL C.693

It may have been his
interest in minerals that led
Beatty to collect Chinese
snuff bottles, many of which
were made from precious or
semi-precious minerals.
The collection now numbers
over 900 but at one time it
exceeded 1,600 as, in later
years, Beatty often gave
away snuff bottles to his
friends as presents.
A related collection of
European snuffboxes was
sold at Sotheby's,
3 December 1962.

Beatty's collection of colour-plate books includes some of the best examples of 19th-century printing, including the works of Joseph Nash (*Views of the Interiors and Exteriors of Windsor Castle*), S Lewis (*Sketches of Spain and Spanish Characters*) and many different works published by Rudolph Ackermann and Edward Orme.

(RIGHT)
HENRY ANDREWS
PAEONIA ALBIFLORA
from Botanist's Repository for new and rare plants
London
T Bensley, 1797

(BELOW RIGHT)
DAVID ROBERTS
TEMPLE AT EDFU
from Egypt and Nubia
London
F G Moon, 1846

This book of hours, executed
for Prigent de Coëtivy
(1400–1450), seen here
praying in his tent, was
purchased by Edith Beatty
in 1919 and presented to
her husband as a present.
The miniatures are attributed
to the "Master of the Duke
of Bedford", who created
many masterpieces for
wealthy patrons.

GRACE BEATTY

Chester Beatty married Grace
Rickard in Denver Cathedral in
1900. They had two children,
Ninette born in 1901 and
Chester junior in 1907. Grace
enjoyed her position as a 5th
Avenue society hostess.
She attended concerts and,
at one time, allowed her name
to be used as a patron of a
concert in aid of the New York
Diet Association. She died of
typhoid fever in 1911.

EDITH BEATTY
Philip de Laszlo (1869-1937)
1916

Edith, Chester Beatty's second
wife, was an important
influence in his life. She had a
wonderful collector's eye and
often suggested purchases for
Beatty. She disdained,
however, Chester Beatty's
preference for the Barbizon
school of painting, preferring
her world-class collection of
French Impressionists. She
died in 1952.

BARODA HOUSE INTERIORS
c.1950

The Edwardian interiors of
the Beattys' London house
were remodelled to reflect
Edith Beatty's passion for
fine French furniture and
over one hundred
Impressionist paintings,
including works by Degas,
Renoir and Van Gogh.

**ILLUMINATED FREEDOM OF
DUBLIN SCROLL**

The Freedom of the City
of Dublin was presented
to Beatty on 7 November
1955 to mark his
benefaction to the city.

THE SUMO WRESTLERS TANIKAZE
AND ONOGAWA
Katsukawa Shunko
(1743–1812)
Woodblock print c.1785
CBL J 2640

FESTIVAL OF THE COCK
The Festival of the Cock
Procession across the Asakusa
Rice Fields
Ando Hiroshige (1797–1858)
Ukiyo-e woodblock print on
paper
1857
CBL J 2695

The Japanese print collection
was one of the last major
areas to be added to the
library. Beatty purchased over
800 examples, mostly in the
1950s and early 1960s,
to form a representative
collection of the genre.

Hiroshige was one of the last
and greatest Japanese print
makers, best known as a
designer of landscape prints.
In his work, he brought
together elements from
Japanese, Chinese and Western
art, and was particularly skilled
at conveying the atmosphere of
climate, season and time of day.
Hiroshige's art was extremely
popular in Europe and America,
where his depictions of nature
influenced artists such as Van
Gogh, Degas and Manet.

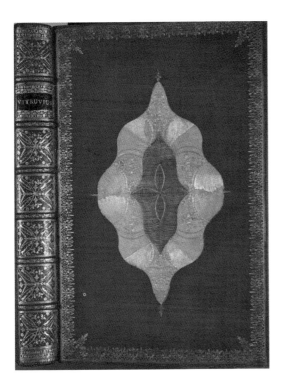 

IRISH BINDINGS
18th century

The Irish bindings in the
Chester Beatty Library include
some of the finest-surviving
examples of many of Ireland's
most accomplished binders.
Beatty was drawn to Irish
bookbinding after his move
to Dublin.

The original Clock Tower
Building in Dublin Castle
appeared on Roque's map of
the city (1756), but the present
structure is a remodelling of the
earlier building by Ireland's
most important early-19th
century architect, Francis
Johnston (d.1829). It became
the new home of the Chester
Beatty Library in 2000.

GEORGE THOMAS,
THE 'RAJA FROM TIPPERARY'
Gold and pigments on paper
c.1820
CBL IN 74.7

Many Irishmen were colonial
administrators in India but
George Thomas became a
favourite of the Begum Samru
of Sardhana, commanding her
army against British regiments.

SULEYMANIYE MOSQUE,
ISTANBUL
from the History of Sultan
Suleyman the Magnificent
Gold and pigments on paper
1579 (dated AH 987)
CBL T 413, f.119

FAKES OR FORGERIES?
CBL Mex 1 (ABOVE)
CBL In. 58.2 (RIGHT)

Collectors are usually aware of unscrupulous individuals who try to sell them forgeries or wrongly attributed works of art. Beatty could often spot many, but his advisors accepted this Mexican painted manuscript as genuine, dating it to 1494. The Indian miniature appears to be early-18th century but it may, in fact, be an image from a much later date. First impressions are not always what they seem and in these examples, scholars disagree as to whether these manuscripts are genuine, defective copies or masterpieces.

PORTRAIT OF
ALFRED CHESTER BEATTY
Colin Colahan (1897–1987)
Oil on canvas
1950

and then the stables of Baroda House into another library. He also housed part of the collection at his country house in Kent. In other respects, too, Beatty's book-collecting activities became more serious: he employed a full-time librarian for the first time, as well as secretaries, and he commissioned scholars to undertake missions to Italy, Germany and Greece to source manuscripts for him. Though tentative at first, delegating the collecting of manuscripts was to become the hallmark of Beatty's collecting technique as he realised that, by employing experts in the field, he could reach sources far wider than the London auction houses and dealers' shops. Perhaps, more importantly for the collector, it gave him the opportunity to acquire items before other collectors became aware of them. Certainly Beatty was not the first collector to employ advisors to form his collection, but he may well have been the first to employ so many. In each field that Beatty ventured into, he referred the manuscripts to advisors for their opinion, whether this was a museum curator or knowledgeable dealer. In this way, Beatty was not only able to compete with other prominent collectors but, in many cases, he was in active competition with the British Museum, the Bibliothèque nationale in Paris and other European national institutions.

By 1922, Beatty was buying heavily from dealers in Paris, Frankfurt, The Hague and London, on a scale that caused concern for his business secretary in New York. To ease concerns, Beatty wrote: "I am economical now and am not buying books as I am trying to accumulate a good bank balance, so you need not be afraid of any big demands from that source." Soon afterwards, however, his company, Selection Trust, began to show results that changed Beatty's fortunes beyond measure as it discovered and controlled the vast output of the Northern Rhodesian Copper Belt. The interiors of Baroda House were completely remodelled in the French 18th-century style to house Mrs Beatty's collection of French furniture and her collection of over a hundred French Impressionist and Post-Impressionist paintings.

THE FOUR HORSEMEN OF THE APOCALYPSE FROM THE REVELATION OF ST JOHN
Woodcut
Nuremberg, 1511
Latin edition
CBL Wep 21

Throughout 1912 and 1913, Beatty was buying heavily enough to be considered an important customer by many London dealers. He was particularly interested in the works of Albrecht Dürer and his followers, especially the German, Dutch and Flemish 'Little Masters'. There are now over 33,000 European prints in the collection.

It was in the 1920s that Beatty's relationship with the British Museum developed and he became an important patron and benefactor. Beatty and his wife, Edith, would often visit the museum where they would be treated as honoured guests. They, in turn, helped the various departments by donating objects or manuscripts, by raising funds for important acquisitions as in the case of the Bedford Book of Hours, Luttrell Psalter and the Codex Sinaiticus. Beatty wanted more, however, and he entered into formal arrangements with many of the curators, paying them annual retainers to advise him of suitable purchases and to catalogue his collection. Today, these contacts would, in many cases, be deemed unethical, or at least questionable, but at the time it was not unusual and many collectors relied on such contacts. Aileen Saarinen, in *The Proud Possessors*, describes J Pierpont Morgan's relationship with the Metropolitan Museum of New York. As its president, Morgan ruled the Metropolitan: "As autocratically and as bent on its success as if it were one of his industrial corporations. He staffed it with the best experts he could find – and then used them as his personal advisors."

The Papyri Collection

Throughout the 1920s and early 1930s, the single most important group of advisors for Beatty included almost all the senior curators in the British Museum's Department of Egyptian Antiquities and allied Cambridge academics. The chief papyri were purchased through dealers, but Beatty's correspondence with Sir Harold Bell shows that Beatty acquired papyri through the museum syndicate, whereby several sponsors of excavations (of whom he was one) distributed the finds among themselves.

By 1925, Beatty was told by Bell that he did not as yet have enough good papyri to warrant a catalogue, to which Beatty replied:

"There is no hurry about the question of my issuing a catalogue, as I intend to pick up during the next two or three years fine examples of papyri, and eventually when I have a more or less comprehensive lot, to throw out the poorer ones, and then bring out a catalogue."[24]

These acquisitions had been made in a fairly unsystematic way, and were generally the rewards for sponsoring British archaeological work in Egypt. Later, in 1928, Alan Gardiner, one of Beatty's other advisors at the British Museum, would chance on a find that would eclipse all of Bell's work for Beatty. Gardiner had discovered that the Cairo dealers were dispersing a collection of ancient Egyptian papyrus rolls and he suggested to Beatty that he should purchase the entire find. Beatty had authorised Gardiner only to acquire items up to £400 and Gardiner's proposal required a far greater investment. He encouraged Beatty further by suggesting, "you will thus acquire a papyrus which is unrivalled in interest in any collection".[25] (The find included an astonishingly well-preserved scroll containing a collection of ancient Egyptian Love Poems dating from 1160 BC.)

Beatty was won over and he authorised Gardiner to acquire as much of the find as possible. After several months of conservation and editing, the Love Poems papyrus was published in a lavish facsimile edition. The content, however, caused Gardiner some concern as he wrote to Beatty: "It is unfortunate that the original story becomes very licentious at this point and I have felt it to be my scientific duty to translate the passages literally as it stands [...] I need not say that the obscene passages were not of my seeking, but imposed by the material."[26] Emery Walker, Beatty's publishers, were also concerned by the sexual nature of the text but agreed to include these passages in the publication as it was noted that the publication would be "an expensive edition which can only appeal to the narrow band of scholars and would not be within reach of the ordinary man".[27]

Even during the financial crisis of late 1929, Beatty, as usual prepared to spend the winter in Cairo. Shortly after their arrival, Beatty toured the usual dealers who had supplied him with manuscripts before. One dealer in particular had acquired a cache of papyrus codices that he now offered for

CONTENDINGS OF HORUS AND SETH/EGYPTIAN LOVE POEMS (DETAIL)
Hieratic text on papyrus c.1160 BC
CBL BP 1

This papyrus scroll contains a number of texts and unusually it has been written on both sides. Apart from a series of business transactions and a text in praise of Rameses V (which helps to date the scroll), the most important text is a series of love poems or songs. These are similar in style to the Song of Solomon found in the Old Testament, where one lover extols the virtues (and physical delights) of the other. Its very early date makes this scroll one of the most important literary scrolls in the world and an extraordinary witness to universal human passions.

ST MARK'S GOSPEL

*From the Four Gospels and
the Acts of the Apostles*
c.AD 250
Greek text on papyrus
CBL BP I (P⁴⁵)

This Chester Beatty papyrus codex is the oldest book in the world to contain these New Testament texts in a single volume. Until its discovery, only small papyrus fragments of single gospels were known. This book showed that the four Gospels and the Acts were compiled into one volume much earlier than many scholars had expected.

sale.[28] Beatty knew that the dealers 'tested the market' before revealing how much of a find they possessed, and bearing in mind his experience with Gardiner and the ancient Egyptian Love Poems, he suspected that what he was shown was only a fraction of what was available. To disguise his interest in the find, Beatty sent a coded telegram to Eric Millar at the British Museum. In reply, and in keeping with Beatty's code, Millar sent the following telegram back to Beatty:

SILVER MINE VERY RICH HAS THREE SHAFTS (STOP)
GOLD MINE RICH HAS FOUR SHAFTS (STOP)
SHOULD BUY BOTH WITHOUT FAIL ESPECIALLY
SILVER MINE (STOP)

Millar sent a copy of the decoded telegram to Beatty's business secretary, John Wooderson, which explained that the 'mines' meant manuscripts, 'rich' meant old and 'shafts' referred to their date. The first manuscript ('silver mine') was 3rd century and the second ('gold mine') 4th century.[29] In short, Beatty's telegram caused a sensation in the British Museum as Millar had sought the advice of the senior curators Kenyon, Bell and Edwards, all of whom had replied that the find was of the greatest importance and interest.[30] This initial purchase was to be followed by many more as Beatty gradually acquired the find, piece by piece. The dealers had split up the books, some quire by quire, others tore the books in half and sold the sections to each other or to collectors. It is thought that Beatty acquired about 90 per cent of the find that included the earliest

THE LETTERS OF ST PAUL
Greek text on papyrus
C.AD 200
CBL Biblical Papyrus II (P[46])

This significant New Testament papyrus contains the text of the Letters of St Paul. Only four other known papyri contain portions of more than one of St Paul's letters, and of these, two are of a much later date. The early date, AD 200, and the fact that it contains almost the complete text of the letters of St Paul, makes this codex extremely important for the study of the text of St Paul's letters.

copies of many New Testament texts as well as some of the earliest copies of the Septuagint (the Greek translation of the Old Testament). When this purchase was made public in *The Times* (19 November 1931), Beatty's fame as a book collector was assured. Letters flooded into Baroda House offering him rare books and manuscripts including one supposedly written "by Jesus". Beatty's papyrus collection was to develop into one of the most important collections in the world, one that no other private collector and few public institutions could match. As he acquired more and more Christian texts, he gave away most of his ancient Egyptian papyri to the British Museum, keeping only one major piece, the Love Poems, and some minor illustrated funerary texts.

The Islamic Collections

Many authors have cited Beatty's first trip to Cairo (December 1913) as the catalyst for his interest in Islamic manuscripts, often painting a picture of him visiting bazaars, 'saving' manuscripts from probable destruction.[31] Such a romantic image is far from the truth, as Beatty's interest in Islamic illumination had been aroused much earlier and his first purchases were made in New York (possibly as early as 1905), Paris (1906) and London (1911).

GEORGE THOMAS, THE
'RAJA FROM TIPPERARY'
(DETAIL, SEE PAGE 27)
c.1820
CBL In 74.7

The interest among collectors in Islamic manuscripts at this time was generally limited to Persian or Mughal illumination and, in this regard, Beatty was no different.[32] Generally only individual items were collected as 'oriental curiosities' and few had embarked on assembling comprehensive collections. Those that had were very often colonial administrators, like Col Henry Hanna (1839–1914), who formed his collection of Mughal and Indian manuscripts while stationed in India. On his return to England in 1887, Hanna exhibited the collection in London and tried unsuccessfully over the next twenty years to sell it, but there was no market for it, even though it was the finest such private collection in England. It was eventually lent to the Laing Art Gallery, Newcastle and, finally in

**THE HISTORY OF SULTAN
SULEYMAN THE MAGNIFICENT**
Persian text
Gold and pigments on paper
1579 (dated AH 987)
CBL T 413

This manuscript, commissioned to record the achievements of Suleyman the Magnificent (reigned 1520–66), depicts many historical events, including the Ottoman conquest of the Balkans.

1907, sold to Charles Freer of Washington for £3,500, half the sum Hanna had expected.[33]

The Hanna collection was sold just before public interest in Mughal art was awakened. In a series of great exhibitions in Paris (1903, 1907, 1912), Munich (1910), London (1912, 1931), and Philadelphia (1926) and New York (1933), the beauty of Islamic illumination was revealed to a wider public. Beatty's now well-established methods of collecting – appraising similar collections in national institutions and employing the best experts – were now applied in earnest to the formation of his Persian, Indian and Ottoman collections. He employed Edgard Blochet, curator of Persian manuscripts at the Bibliothèque nationale in Paris and entered into joint-purchase arrangements with the British Museum and the Victoria & Albert Museum in order to secure some of the best pieces that came up for auction. The major book dealers in London and Paris were now searching for suitable acquisitions for Beatty and, in 1923, Quaritch's obtained a portion of a Mughal manuscript that they knew Beatty could not refuse. The manuscript was the *Akbarnama*, an early-17th century chronicle of the reign of Akbar the Great (reigned 1556–1605), with over fifty exquisite miniatures.[34] It was purchased for $5,000.

Like his earlier purchases, Beatty only bought items on approval, as he knew that modern hands had over-painted many of the miniatures. This resulted in hundreds of books, miniatures and print albums being sent to Baroda House. Beatty's secretaries carefully noted the contents of each book, the price requested and Beatty's comments on each item, which more often than not, were a curt, "No good, fetched away", or a dismissive abbreviation such as "DCI", for 'don't care for it'. Occasionally Beatty would be more expressive: "The book mentioned duly arrived and I am returning it to you as it is not important enough for me. I am only interested in very artistic and fine manuscripts of outstanding quality."[35] Beatty had now established his market price for Mughal miniatures, paying an average £200 for good examples and £300 if they were signed. The collection drew admiration from many people including a discreet notice in the Court Circular (9 March 1939), which reported that Queen Mary had visited Baroda House to see Mr Beatty's collection of Indian miniatures. The press now reported that "Mr Beatty has

EMPEROR AKBAR AND THE JESUITS
*From the History of Akbar
(Akbarnama)
Persian text on paper
c. 1605*
CBL In 3 f.263

brought together a collection such as cannot have been in one library since the fall of the Mughal Empire, for it surpasses even that in the Bibliothèque nationale in the splendour of illumination and the quality of the miniature painting".[36]

In 1935, Beatty told his friend and fellow collector, Sir Robert Abdy, "I do not like buying anything anymore. Occasionally I pick up a rare book while I am in Egypt but my purchases are practically finished." Nevertheless, his collecting activities continued; existing collections were expanded and new areas of interest developed. The methods he had employed previously, engaging advisors and 'scouts', were to have spectacular results, leading to a doubling of the collection, particularly in the area of Arabic rare texts. In fact, the rate of expansion had to be reduced, as the scholars employed to compile the catalogues could not keep up with the flow of manuscripts. The source of these additions was mostly the Middle East and, in one year alone, Beatty acquired nearly 1,000 manuscripts, the cost of which was carefully worked out at five Egyptian pounds each. The rooms in Baroda House and Calehill Park could no longer hold the collection, and his librarian politely complained about the inappropriate storage of some items, particularly his famous Egyptian Love Poems that had to be kept under a settee.

Beatty and Ireland

At the outbreak of World War II, Beatty transferred many of the treasures of Baroda House to America, but kept most of his library in Kent. Although some scholars continued to catalogue the collection, Beatty's attention was totally devoted to the war effort. By the late 1940s, however, Beatty had become disillusioned with Britain, finding the recently elected Labour government's bureaucratic policies not to his liking. He decided to move to Ireland, explaining to the *Daily Express*, "It will be pleasanter to drink a glass of Irish beer in a Dublin garden than to spend the rest of my life buying fountain pens and filling in forms."[37] Just as Britain was starting to rebuild after the war, Beatty's move to Ireland caused a sensation in British financial circles, as it was feared that other prominent industrialists might follow his example. Indeed, it was for this very reason that the Irish civil servants of the time encouraged Beatty to make the move.

In 1950, when he left London and moved to Ireland, Beatty was seventy-five years old. He was welcomed in a way that many would find unacceptable today. He received special treatment from the government, not least of all, exemption from the strict foreign exchange rules, which limited the amount of money people could take out of the country. He also secured the waiving of import taxes on purchases for his library but, more importantly, because Beatty wanted to ensure that his library would remain intact, he arranged that his books and manuscripts and other library property would receive preferential treatment after his death. These were no small financial concessions in the post-war era, but they secured for Ireland, not only the Chester Beatty Library, but also Beatty's patronage of the National Gallery of Ireland, the Military Museum at the Curragh, as well as thousands of pounds in donations to hospitals and medical charities.

PRESENTATION OF FIRST HONORARY CITIZENSHIP TO BEATTY, 7 AUGUST 1957
(l–r: Éamon de Valera (Taoiseach), Sean T Ó Ceallaigh (President of Ireland), Alfred Chester Beatty and John A Costello (Leader of the Opposition)

The two great passions in Chester Beatty's life, his mining interests and his library, brought him fame and fortune. In recognition of his charitable works, he received honours and awards from many countries as well as from academic and cultural institutions. He received a knighthood from Queen Elizabeth II in 1954, the Freedom of the City of Dublin in 1956 and, in 1957, he was made the first Honorary Citizen of Ireland. In 1999, he was posthumously recognised by the National Mining Hall of Fame in Leadville, Colorado.

When Beatty moved to Ireland, he brought with him not only his collection but also his librarian, publisher, bank manager and book restorer. He bought a large town house in the Ballsbridge area of Dublin and set about looking for a suitable site to house his library. After looking at several establishments in the city, Beatty decided to purchase a site near to his own home. Architects were appointed and Beatty's librarian looked to American models for establishing the new Chester Beatty Library on Shrewsbury Road. He liked the idea of creating a haven for scholarship set in formal gardens. Even at this late stage in his life, Beatty continued to collect books, but this time he sought items that he thought would appeal to his friend Éamon de Valera and Catholic Ireland. He purchased many 16th-century Jesuit publications, particularly items relating to the Jesuit missions to China, Japan and India, numerous illustrated copies of the Ethiopian text of the Miracles of the Virgin Mary and over fifty Greek and Russian icons.

Apart from building the Chester Beatty Library and adding to the collection, Beatty also concentrated on publishing his collection. He commissioned a variety of international scholars to come to Dublin to catalogue the Armenian, Slavonic, Batak, Tibetan, Mongolian and Arabic texts. He also established The Chester Beatty Monographs, a series that published detailed descriptions of individual manuscripts in the collection. Even though the administration of the library and all the publication costs were paid for by Beatty, he still managed to add to the collection. The last major area he developed was the Japanese Print Collection, and over 800 examples of Japanese woodblock prints from the 18th and 19th centuries were purchased in the late-1950s and early-1960s.

The foundation of Beatty's library had been laid in America, but its transformation had occurred in the London of the 1920s and 1930s. Beatty was then one of the richest men in Britain, ranked alongside the 'Rand Lords', those new millionaires who had made their fortunes in South African gold and diamond mines. After World War II, Beatty could no longer collect manuscripts and printed books to the standard that he had set himself. There were now fewer fine manuscripts available, other collectors were entering the fields that Beatty once had to himself, and prices were beginning to rise.

Unlike some of his contemporaries, Beatty had no grand plan when he was forming his collection, or, if he did, it has remained firmly hidden. He collected over a long period of sixty years compared to the twenty years that Morgan and Huntington spent amassing their libraries. In contrast to these 'titans', Beatty was never prepared to compete openly in the auction rooms, and whereas J Pierpont Morgan believed that "no price is too high for an object of unquestioned beauty and known authenticity", Beatty was more circumspect. Even when urged by his librarian to spend a little more on an acquisition as "one real prize is worth twenty good ones", Beatty was restrained; assembling his collection quietly and at first without much public notice. His reticence at paying very high prices may have dissuaded Beatty from purchasing a first folio of Shakespeare or a Gutenburg Bible but, if he felt any regret, it was never mentioned. He felt compensated by his ownership of some of the earliest manuscripts of the Christian Gospels and some of the most beautiful books every produced.

Chester Beatty died in 1968 after a long and eventful life, leaving a fortune, conservatively estimated at £186 million. Four years later, Chester Beatty Jr. sold his father's company, Selection Trust, for £400 million but, for many, Beatty's greatest legacy is now one of Ireland's national cultural institutions, grant-aided by the State and owned by a public charitable trust. The public galleries, which display about 1 per cent of the collection, show the evolution of the book from ancient times to the present, and the library continues to attract scholars from all over the world who come to study the rare texts and illuminated manuscripts. For Beatty, from 'mucker' to 'Copper King', it had all been a great adventure.

THE OLD CHESTER BEATTY LIBRARY, SHREWSBURY ROAD, DUBLIN
"I have always wanted to found a library for Dublin more or less on the lines of the great Morgan Library in New York. Dublin is a city of wonderful culture and art consciousness."
Alfred Chester Beatty on the opening of his library, *Irish Independent,* 12 August 1950.

Further Reading

The Chester Beatty Library website (www.cbl.ie) contains more information on the Western, Islamic and East Asian sections of the collection as well as details of events in the library.

Chester Beatty Library [Scala Guide] (London: Scala Publishers, 2001).

Horton, Charles, " 'It was all a great adventure': Alfred Chester Beatty and the formation of his Library" *History Ireland* 8 No. 2 (2000) pp. 37–42.

Kennedy, Brian, *Alfred Chester Beatty and Ireland: A Study in Cultural Politics 1950–1968* (Dún Laoghaire: Glendale Press, 1988).

Ushioda, Yoshiko, *Tales of Japan: Three Centuries of Japanese Painting from the Chester Beatty Library, Dublin* (Alexandria, VA: Art Services International, 1992).

Wilson, A J, *The Life and Times of Sir Alfred Chester Beatty* (London: Cadogan Publications, 1985).

1. Beatty is not listed in either, Carl L Cannon, *American Book Collectors and Collecting: From Colonial Times to the Present* (New York: H W Wilson, 1941), or Donald C Dickinson, *Dictionary of American Book Collectors* (New York: Greenwood Press, 1986), while Seymour de Ricci makes only a passing reference to Beatty in *English Collectors of Books and Manuscripts 1500–1930* (Cambridge: Cambridge University Press, 1930) p. 172.

2. A quotation by Montague Rhodes James bemoaning the dispersal of the Yates Thompson collection to non-English collectors. See Josiah Q Bennett, "Portman Square to New Bond Street or How to Make Money though Rich" *The Book Collector* 16 (1967) p. 325.

3. Beatty was a member of the Sons of the Revolution and the General Society of Colonial Wars. These patriotic societies were established to "perpetuate the memory" of the founders of the United States and, in particular, to reverse "the steady decline of a proper celebration of the National Holidays of the United States of America". See websites: General Society of Colonial Wars (www.ubait.edu/gscw/preamble) and Sons of the Revolution (www.amrev.org/htaocs/html/fm/homepg). Beatty became a naturalised British citizen in 1933 and, during World War II, helped to organise the United Kingdom Corporation Ltd, which helped to source raw materials for the war effort.

4. "I like to think that the English and Scottish strains helped him to make money and the Irish strain helped him to spend it," commented Richard Hayes (Chester Beatty's librarian) in his opening address at an exhibition of Chester Beatty manuscripts at Princeton University, February 1967. Chester Beatty Papers. Correspondence between Richard Hayes and Princeton University (16 February 1965–12 December 1967).

5. There are two unpublished biographies of Chester Beatty, one compiled by Richard Hayes, Director of the National Library of Ireland, the other by a Dublin journalist, John Murdoch. Substantial parts of Murdoch's version appeared in A J Wilson, *The Life and Times of Sir Alfred Chester Beatty* (London: Cadogan, 1985).

6. Chester Beatty Papers. Murdoch, Biography, p. 5.

7. Wilde descended to the mine face standing on a bucket – this was still the method of descent when Beatty worked at Cripple Creek, Colorado. See Richard Ellmann, *Oscar Wilde* (London: Penguin Books, 1987) pp. 181, 193–194.

8. John Hays Hammond, *The Autobiography of John Hays Hammond* 2 vols (New York: Ferrar & Rinehart, 1935) p. 483.

9. Robert Hoe III was a printing-press manufacturer and next to J Pierpont Morgan, America's greatest book collector. His sale was the most important book sale in American history. See: Edwin Wolf II & John Fleming, *Rosenbach: A Biography* (London: Weidenfeld & Nicholson, 1960) p. 72.

10. Wolf & Fleming, *ibid.*, p. 103.

11. For Huntington's objective, see Donald C Dickinson, *Henry E Huntington's Library of Libraries* (San Marino, Ca.: Huntington Library Press, 1995) pp. xv–xvii. Morgan's objective is described in Louis Auchincloss, *J P Morgan: The Financier as Collector* (New York: Harry N Abrams Inc., Publishers, 1990) p. 54. Henry Clay Folger's aims are described in Frederick A Bearman *et al.*, *Fine and Historic Bookbindings from the Folger Shakespeare Library* (Washington DC: The Folger Shakespeare Library, 1992) p. 5.

12. Robert Allan Shaddy, "'A Mad World, My Master!' Book Collecting in America, 1890–1930" (unpublished doctoral thesis, University of Missouri-Columbia, December 1990) p. 17. For some theories on collecting see, Werner Muensterberger, *Collecting an Unruly Passion: Psychological Perspectives* (Princeton, New Jersey: Princeton University Press, 1994). Susan M Pearce (ed.), *On Collecting. An Investigation into Collecting in the European Tradition* (London and New York: Routledge, 1995).

13. Douglas & Elizabeth Rigby, *Lock, Stock and Barrel: the Story of Collecting* (New York: Lippincott, 1944) pp. 3–82 quoted in Shaddy, *ibid.*, p. 33.

14. Chester Beatty Papers. Newspaper Cuttings Book. *The Times* [no date but c. 1965].

15. US government Revenue Act of 1897. J Pierpont Morgan estimated that it would cost him $3 million in tax to transfer his collection from London to New York. It had been stored at his house at Prince's Gate and Dover House just outside London and many items were on loan to the Victoria & Albert Museum.

16. Auchincloss, *op. cit.*, p.85.

17. The major New York book sales of the period began with the Hoe sale in 1911 and continued with those of the Huntington duplicates, Hagen, Vernon and Jones collections up to 1919. The London sales included the Fairfax Murray and Yates Thompson collections. See: Wolf & Fleming, *op. cit.*, p. 73 and p. 110.

18. The sale, by the Anderson Auction Company, even attracted Alfred Quaritch and Ernest Maggs from London. The bids were lower at the second Hoe sale in 1912, perhaps in reaction to adverse public comment. The third sale started the morning the news of the *Titanic* tragedy broke. See: Wolf & Fleming, *op. cit.*, p.73 and p.110.

19. Christopher de Hamel, "Cockerell and Chester Beatty" *Hidden Friends:* A Loan Exhibition of the Comites Latentes Collection of Illuminated Manuscripts from the Bibliothèque Publique et Universitaire, Geneva, 20–28 September 1985 (London: Sotheby's & Co., 1985).

20. Chester Beatty Papers. "Western Mss. Old General Catalogue VIII–XVIII Century" p. 1.

21. This description cannot be positively identified with library lists and it may be a previous attribution to the Chester Beatty Rosarium or Prayer Book of Phillip II of Spain with miniatures by Simon Bening (CBL Ms W99). Recent scholarship has revealed that this manuscript belonged to Phillip's father, Emperor Charles V.

22. Purchased "privately from Mr Yates Thompson and presented to me by my wife June 21st, 1919". Cost: "EKKK" [£4,000] Chester Beatty Papers. "Western MSS. Old General Catalogue VIII–XVIII Century", no. 87. Now Chester Beatty Library, Mss W82.

23. Chester Beatty Papers. Correspondence between Beatty and Martin Nijhoff (21 Jul 1919–14 Mar 1924). This is the earliest statement of Beatty's preferences found to date.

24. Chester Beatty Papers. Beatty to Bell, 6 July 1925.

25. Chester Beatty Papers. Gardiner to Beatty, 28 March 1928.

26. Chester Beatty Papers. Gardiner to Beatty, 8 April 1928.

27. Chester Beatty Papers. Emery Walker to John Johnson, 23–26 January 1931.

28. German academics also knew of the find and they attempted to secure it "but the dealers, scenting a killing, put up their prices beyond the reach of any but a millionaire". See G S Wegener, *6000 Years of the Bible* trans by Margaret Shenfield (London: Hodder & Stoughton, 1963) p. 90.

29. Chester Beatty Papers. Millar, 3 February 1930. This telegram relates to the purchase of Chester Beatty Biblical Papyri VII, a 3rd-century papyri codex of the Book of Daniel and Chester Beatty Biblical Papyri VI, a 4th-century copy of the Book of Genesis.

30. On Beatty's return to London, Bell wrote of the purchase, "all [are] Biblical or religious, which personally I regret, as I should have liked texts of great literature", but added that the find "must certainly rank with the most important ever made". Chester Beatty Papers. Bell to Beatty, 11 April 1930.

31. In several interviews when he was in his nineties, Beatty mentions 1913 as the start of his collecting, even though substantial purchases were made before this date. "When my wife and I took a trip to Egypt in 1913, I spent a lot of time in the souks and bought a few papyri that turned out to be important. I also saw some decorated Korans that seemed remarkable." Chester Beatty to Lady Powerscourt quoted in Sheila Powerscourt, *Sun Too Fast* (London, Geoffrey Bles, 1974) p. 230.

32. For a study on the rise of Islamic collections in the West, see Stephan Roman, "The Development of Islamic Library Collections in Western Europe and North America" in Muntaz A Anwar (ed.), *Libraries and Librarianship in the Muslim World* (London: Mansell, 1990).

33. See Thomas Lawton & Linda Merrill, *Freer: A Legacy of Art* (Washington DC; The Freer Art Gallery, 1992).

34. Now Dublin, Chester Beatty Library Ms In 3. Another large section of this manuscript is in the British Library and several individual pages in various collections.

35. Chester Beatty Papers. Beatty to J Acheroff (Dealer, Cairo and Paris), 2 January 1929.

36. *Burlington Magazine*, March 1939.

37. For Beatty's decision to move his collection to Ireland, see Brian P Kennedy, *Alfred Chester Beatty and Ireland 1950–1968: A Study in Cultural Politics* (Dún Laoghaire: The Glendale Press, 1988) pp. 41–64.